Copyright © 2010

Published by
Ceipub Division of Circle of Entertainment Incorporated
PO box 25091 Brooklyn, NY 11202
Office 718-930-4220

Credits:
Illustration and Design by James Paul
Copy edit by Robert Young

Special thanks:
L. Aldridge, C. Rousseau, M. Stewart, R.Stuart

Made and printed in the U.S.A.
Isbn-13: 978-0-9845320-0-1   Isbn-10: 0-9845320-0-5

100 GHETTO Golden Rules

BY PANTA WILSON

ILLUSTRATION AND DESIGN BY JAMES M PAUL

1

If you don't have enough muscles to beat your wife, um, don't wear a wife beater.

2

If you have a big, flabby stomach. When you rock that big belt to hide it, guess what? We can still see your big flabby stomach underneath it.

3

If you buy your designer accessories
(Guccis, Vuttons and Pradas) off the street.
The second you turn the key to your
project rent stabilized apartment,
we know it's fake.

4

Ladies, please don't wear open toe sandals, open toe heels or open toe anything if your feet look like camels.

5

Ladies, don't wear booty shorts if you not gonna lotion the bottom of your cheeks. It just looks like you've been sitting in snow since the winter and summer caught you off guard.

6

Ladies, stop wearing no clothes in freezing temperatures. Next time you go out, read the sign: This club is not responsible for inappropriate dress codes: micro mini skirts, short shorts, open toe stilettos in the snow, or wearing no coat on the line because you're too cheap to pay for coat check may cause pneumonia. Enter at your own risk!

7

If you can't afford a pedicure, there is still no excuse for rough foot heels. There is an invention called the potato peeler. Use it.

8

If you don't have any nail on your pinky toe, just leave it alone. Do not attempt to disguise it by painting the top of your toe into the shape of a nail. You're not fooling anyone.

9

Baby wipes are to freshen up a clean kitty kat, not clean a dirty one.

10

If you're planning to come over for sex ladies, do not, I repeat do not take a dump right before you leave your house, because when you bend over, we can still smell your crusty ass.

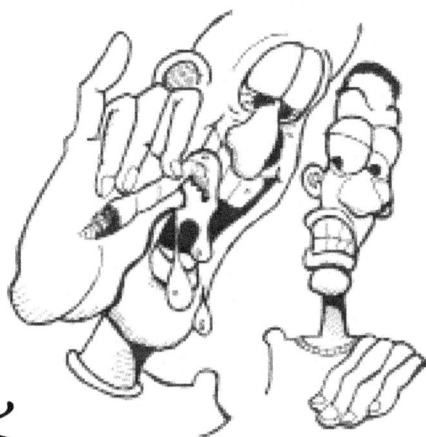

11

Fellaz, if you ever smoked a blunt after your man just finished using his tongue and saliva to roll it up. That is officially an indirect french kiss and you may have just experienced your first gay encounter. Next time you may wanna think before you puff puff pass.

12

Ladies, be cautious when you decide to get a "Tramp Stamp" because when you hit 70. What are you going to tell your grand kids when they ask nana "Why do (you) have (to) lick it before you stick it tattooed on your lower back"?

13

Ladies, if your real hair looks like a rough grain of sand paper, do not go out and buy a silky smooth weave and try to blend it in, to create a more natural look; it's not working! You just need to stop!

14

Fellaz, it may be trendy to rock a pair of skinny jeans but when you have to wiggle into them or the thought crosses your mind to borrow a pair from your sister or girlfriend, it may be time to abort. By the way, can guys get yeast infections?

15

Even if you have the prettiest feet in the world and you get pedicures 5 times a week. If you're not 3 inches from a pool, Fellaz, under no circumstances should you have a desire to show off your toes. That means keep them joints covered. No open toe sandals, no thong flip flops and no see thru timberland boots. I don't think they make those but if they do, we don't want to see your damn toes in those either.

16

To my jocks; if your teammate scores a goal in any sport, never, I mean never, congratulate him by giving him a tap on the ass!

17

If you're at the urinal, do not attempt to strike up a conversation with the man next to you, about anything. Now is not the time! Finish yo leak, get your three shakes, leave the premises and don't forget to wash yo nasty hands, cuz I know you gonna try to give someone a pound lata on.

18

We have been stuffing things in our pockets for years. Since when has it become cool to carry around a man purse?

19

If your belly looks like a Buddha or has so many stretch marks that only a male zebra will find you attractive, please don't wear a belly ring, a belly shirt or a belly nothing, thank you very much.

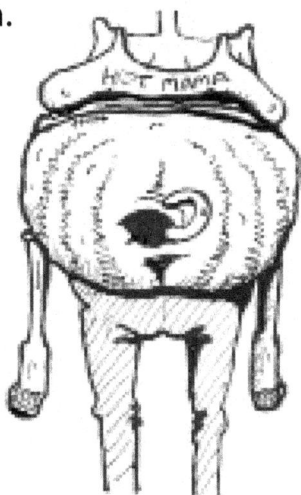

20

If you only have one good outfit. Stop allowing photographers to post your pic on their party sites. You're confusing the hell out of me. I am starting to think this week's party is last week's, cuz there you go again with your same old outfit and changing the color of your socks does not make it a new outfit.

21

My older sister was known as the smart one and my older brother was known as the athlete but when you're the baby of the family, you're just known as the remote.

22

Just because you say you know what
I'm saying a million times doesn't mean
we know what you're saying. Nah what I
mean?

23

If your mama made you when she was 15, you can't hate on your boyfriend if he wants to do her, y'all practically sisters.

24

If you drive a hundred thousand dollar luxury car, should you really be concerned about alternate side street parking rules?

25

If you're over 30 and live at home with your moms, you should be abstinent. That's it!

26

If you have 2 kids or more from a previous relationship, that's not baggage; that's luggage!

27

Gold Diggers; if he came in your mouth
and you swallowed .... you can not take
him to court for child support! You need
to regroup, think it over and come up with
another get rich plan.

28

Why is it every time you holla at a dime piece, her fat ugly friend always wants to jump in? Well, we're not talking to you! Your job is to hold the purses and the coats while your good looking friends get their groove on.

29

"Alumni" does not mean going back to your old high school years later to bag young freshman girls.

30

Do not think by putting Lamborghini style doors on your civic, that it disguises the fact that you're driving a hooptie. In fact, all it does is draw more attention to how much of a loser you really are.

31

Instead of getting six mobile phones to look important, why don't you try getting a secretary?

32

Making it rain with single dollar bills is like comparing morning dew to a tropical rain storm.

33

Six men chipping in and nursing one bottle of champagne at the club, does not equal balling.

34

The refrigerator was invented to store food, not recharge your AAA batteries.

35

If your braids or hairline start at the back of your neck, it might be a good time to start rocking a baldy, cuz right now, you just look ridiculous.

36

Paper plates are for one time use only! Do not attempt to wash them and hang them out to dry.

37

If you don't sign autographs for a living,
please do not wear your sunglasses at
night or at any indoor facilities.

38

Weave, make up, contacts, fake nails, girdles, push up bras and implants. Do they even make real women anymore?

39

If you suffer from "noazzatall", don't go out there and buy yo self a pair of apple bottom jeans. False advertisement is not cute.

40

I heard of "Fake it till you make it" but can we stop with the fake bling? I, for one, am starting to get a rash just looking at you. Secondly, who the hell are you trying to attract with a ton of scrap metal around your neck, besides a magnet and lastly our ancestors lost their lives trying to get out of chains! Why the hell are you trying so hard to get back into them?

41

If your child knows how to recite their favorite rap song before they can recite their A B C's, count to ten or spell their name correctly, I am personally reporting you to one of the child protective agencies.

42

If you've been hustling on the block for years and have nothing to show for it. Breaking news you are not a hustler!!!

43

If you're going to commit a crime, at least make sure the crime you commit covers the bail money, duh.

44

Hood breaking news alert!!!! Pit Bulls and Rottweilers are not the only breeds of dogs that exist on earth.

45

If you're going on a job interview, black
work boots are not a substitute for shoes.

46

If you're living in a trailer park, wouldn't it be wiser to drive to a better neighborhood and park up there?

47

Never use a money clip to hold your food stamps!

48

If you tell your guest your kitchen faucet has a built in juice dispenser. They won't question you when you serve them brown water.

49

What's the difference between a community swimming pool and a public restroom? For your sake, I hope that deep yellow tint in the water is actually chlorine.

50

Just because you have a thousand Facebook friends doesn't mean you're popular in real life.

51

A single family home means just that. It is not designed for your entire extended family to live with you.

52

Magnum XL condoms are not meant to have a baggy fit. If you are experiencing this, you may need to downsize.

53

Ladies, food may be the way to a man's heart but the corns on your toes should be left off the menu.

54

Pissy hallways, pissy stairs and pissy elevators. Is there some unknown bladder epidemic that prevents hood folks from making it upstairs to the bathrooms that comes with the apartment?

55

If you saved all the money you spent on trying to win the lotto, you would be a millionaire already.

56

Serving jail time is not a badge of honor. It just means you did something wrong and was stupid enough to get caught.

57

Now that we have cell phones and door bells with intercoms, can you please stop yelling outside my window? Sigh!

58

Who do you think you're fooling walking around with a wad of cash that you just got from your income tax return? If you really want people to think you're rich, try walking around with an American express black card.

59

If your man has been calling you wifey for over 5 years. Get a clue bitch! He's not marrying you. You're just his jump off.

60

Ladies, if your man always has to use his own hand to finish off. Your head game is wack!

61

Ladies, your man is not cheap. He just doesn't have enough money left from spending it on his real girlfriend.

62

Ladies, learn the difference between a phat azz and a fat ass. Fat will never be the new thick.

63

I just don't get gold teeth. Why would anyone think making your teeth more yellow is attractive? Walking around like a gingivitis patient is not cute.

64

What happens when you run out of kool aid mix? By all means, make yourself a tall refreshing glass of sugar water.

65

If you're going to buy bottle water, please don't serve it with tap water ice cubes.

66

Wearing your pants around your knees to show off your butt? Wait a sec fellaz, when did this become gangster? It looks more like you're heading to an audition for gay porn.

67

Can somebody please invent a masculine way for men to apply lip balm?

68

Can I get evicted if I forgot to list the roaches and rats as occupants on my lease agreement?

69

The iron is the most multifunction invention. Not only can it press a shirt but it also makes one hell of a grilled cheese sandwich.

70

Just because you've became an expert at cutting the toothpaste open when it's done, doesn't mean it will guarantee you a spot in med school.

71

Can someone show me where does it say please add water to ketchup bottle when finished?

72

Who needs a fireplace when the place comes with a perfectly working kitchen oven?

73

How can you complain if you received a bad copy of a bootleg DVD? Hey dumb ass, a bootleg is a bad copy.

74

Everyone knows that your high water dress pants will eventually end up being the third piece of your little brother's graduation suit.

75

Can you stop asking people "How you doing?" when you and I both know you would care less if they dropped dead right in front of you?

76

Purple lips and burnt finger tips. Hmmmm. Do you really think no one has a clue that you're a bonafide WEED HEAD!!!

_77_

Hey parents, can you at least wait until your
3 year old child can drive before you put
the car notes in their name?

78

If you spent more time using your toothbrush to clean your teeth instead of cleaning your sneakers, you wouldn't walk around with bad breath.

79

There is a good reason why they call it a mansion. Um, men, can we get back to being the head of the household?

80

"My bad" and "Bling Bling" died years ago.
Don't you read the obituary pages?

81

Fellaz, if you're attracted to female body-builders, why don't you just get straight to the point and start dating men?

82

The panhandlers nowadays look like they have more money than the people they're begging from. I think it's time for a career change.

83

If you're going to date outside of your race, that is not a reason to pretend you're blind. Your mate still has to look cute.

84

If you can't spell it or pronounce it, don't eat it!

85

Never take a happy meal girl to a five star restaurant unless you plan on ordering two cups of embarrassment.

86

Stop naming your kids after cars you can't buy. While Mercedes and Lexus may be out of your league, Hyundai and Kia are just as good names.

87

Let's just hope chickens never come into power because we all know the first race they're going to seek revenge on.

88

Don't pay your cable bill before you pay your rent unless you plan on watching TV outside.

89

They should start putting addresses on the street corners. At least that way, it will be a lot quicker to find out where your friends really live.

90

I hope you still think it's cute in 10 years when your 8 year old daughter is doing those same dances she learned from the music videos in a smelly night club for one buck.

91

Now that you've added a ton of black music on your playlist, don't you think it's time to add some black people to your contact list?

92

If you don't own multiple homes and you're not a janitor … why are you walking around town with a bunch of keys on your key ring?

93

How can you moon someone if you don't have an ass? Isn't it more like a lunar eclipse?

94

We already have a minimum age requirement to get in the club but I think we need to add a maximum because something ain't right about a 100 year old man asking a 18 year old for a dance.

95

Why do we pay designers to wear their logo? If you're going to become a walking billboard, shouldn't they be cutting you a check for outstanding advertising and promotions?

96

Why does "Let me get four wings" translate into 42 different words when you're ordering Chinese food? Can you imagine if you tried to add fries to that?

97

Stop patting your head to death. Just listen…. that's just your hair saying "Hey stupid, please take this nasty weave off my head and wash me".

98

One million dollars to whoever can explain why do women shave off their eyebrows only to draw them back on with a pencil?

99

For many, the birth of a disabled child can be devastating but in the hood, that's a steady check for life.

100

Reading street tales, romance novels and this book does not give you the right to call yourself a scholar.

About the author

Panta A. Wilson was born and raised in Brooklyn, NY. Despite growing up in one of the toughest inner city neighborhoods, he managed to escape through education and obtain a bachelors degree in Business Administration.

There is certainly a bleak overtone in the inner city, but ironically within the same environment lies some of the most humorous and unorthodox perceptions on life. That is exactly what the author wanted to share with the rest of the world.